40 DAYS OF DEVOTIONS FOR TEEN GIRLS

No Filter

written by

1 GIRL NATION

Requests for permission should be addressed in writing to LifeWay Press®, One LifeWay Plaza, Nashville, TN 37234-0144.

ISBN: 978-1-4300-4159-7
Item Number: 005737737
Dewey Decimal Classification Number: 248.83
Subject Heading: GIRLS \ FAITH \ SPIRITUAL LIFE

Printed in the United States of America

Student Ministry Publishing
LifeWay Church Resources

One LifeWay Plaza
Nashville, TN 37234-0144

Table of Contents

About 1 Girl Nation

Talent, passion, and youthful exuberance are always a potent recipe for great music, but when you add message driven lyrics, a finely tuned sense of purpose, and four fun-loving girls, therein lays the foundation for an explosive new entry on the cultural landscape. 1 Girl Nation (1GN) is made up of four talented young women, each possessing a strong, distinctive voice and tons of personality. Together they deliver an ear-grabbing, effervescent sound that uplifts audiences by merging engaging melodies with substantive yet catchy lyrics. Their songs carry powerful messages about finding identity in Christ as well as encouraging people to lean on God during times of struggle.

Lindsey Adamec

Lindsey is a Pastor's kid hailing from Jacksonville, FL. She grew up singing in church and leading worship at camps and conferences. After recording her independent EP, Lindsey auditioned and was selected for 1 Girl Nation. When not touring, she enjoys hanging out on the beach, spending time with her brothers, and shopping. She married her high school sweetheart, Austin, in the summer of 2014.

Carmen Justice

Carmen is a singer/dancer from Nashville, TN, where she studied music at the famed Belmont University. She has been dancing all of her life, and now creates all of the choreography for 1 Girl Nation. In her free time, Carmen enjoys writing music, dancing, hanging out with friends, and she can often be found at the neighborhood "hipster" coffee house reading and enjoying her favorite beverage. Carmen is known for her ability to laugh and make people feel "joy" and is preparing now to spend the rest of her life with her best friend, Matt.

Kayli Robinson

Kayli lived all over the world while her father served in the U.S. Air Force. She and her family eventually settled in Orlando, FL. She graduated with a Bachelors degree in Church Ministry focusing in Music and Psychology from Southwestern Assemblies of God University. She enjoys watching movies and being at home with her family as much as she can. Kayli loves high fashion and can be found in coffee shops reading from her favorite fashion blogs and finding the best ways to shop for less.

Lauryn Taylor Bach

Lauryn Taylor is a singer/songwriter from Birmingham, AL, where she still resides today. She began her music career through the Artist Development program at the Nashville-based PCG Institute (Premiere Career Guidance). Lauryn Taylor loves to play guitar, rap, and embrace her inner hippy! When she is off stage, she enjoys spending time with her family, writing songs, and watching movies in her onesie.

About No Filter

In a culture obsessed with picture perfect moments, it's tempting to present only the best of ourselves to the world around us. We put filters on our images, brush away imperfections, and anxiously await affirmation from others. But this is not how we were created to live. We were made to thrive in the freedom of grace. We were made to shine in the light of infinite love. We were made to live beautifully authentic lives. Only when we see ourselves through the lens of God's truth can we truly know what it means to walk this journey with confidence and purpose.

In this 40-day devotional, teen girls will get a glimpse into the lives of 1 Girl Nation as Lindsey, Carmen, Kayli, and Lauryn Taylor share what they have discovered about life, love, identity, faith, and so much more. The common theme running through their stories is how their relationship with Christ has taught them to live with authenticity. Their hope is that more girls will discover the freedom of living with no filter.

DAY
1

More than Enough

God's Word is filled with letters that describe His great love for us. If we could see ourselves the way Jesus sees us, we would never look at ourselves the same!

If you struggle in this area, you are not alone. I'm right there with you. It's a daily battle not to fall for the lies Satan whispers to my heart. For the longest time I believed those lies. Insecurity ate me up inside. I would look at myself in the mirror and critique my appearance for hours asking God, "Why did you make me this way?" The Enemy would tell me I wasn't beautiful, I was unloveable, I wouldn't amount to anything. I would never be enough. And sadly, I believed every word.

Because I believed the lies, I let that distorted view of myself define me. I started dating guys who treated me horribly, because I thought that's what I deserved. I would skip meals and even make myself throw up, because I believed a lower number on the scale would somehow give me more worth. I was broken and felt alone, until God in His faithfulness intervened. He brought the right people into my life at just the right time who recognized the battle I was fighting and pointed me to the source of victory. They encouraged

Lindsey

me to look into God's Word to see what my Creator says about me; to find out how <u>the One who designed me defines my value</u> and identity. What I discovered changed my life!

Because I now know the freedom of complete acceptance, I can more easily recognize the lies of Satan when I hear them. My prayer is that if you struggle in this area, you will learn to stand on the truth of God's Word and resist the Enemy's trap.

Maybe you think this battle in your mind isn't a big deal, or maybe you are completely overwhelmed by it. Either way, your self-worth is at stake and you must learn to fight. Look at it from a different angle—if someone threatened you physically, you wouldn't sit back and casually deal with the situation. NO! You would kick and scream and fight for your life, right? Well the same goes for how you deal with Satan. When he is whispering those lies that you are not enough, you need to stand up and fight for your identity and freedom! <u>Victory comes through the Word of God.</u> His truth is all that matters and it is wrapped up in this reality: when Jesus died on the cross, He invited you into a relationship that totally redefines your past, present, and future. His love and acceptance is what makes you beautiful and gives your life infinite value!

Choose to believe what God says about you. You are MORE than enough because you are <u>loved by your Creator and Savior.</u>

The LORD your God is in your midst, a mighty one who will save; he will rejoice over you with gladness; he will quiet you by his love, he will exult over you with loud singing.

ZEPHANIAH 3:17 (ESV)

DAY
2

Lonliness

I am a writer by nature. I love processing life through the power of words. I enjoy recording those words in my journal so I can look back at where I've been and what I've learned.

I love that feeling when I get to the end of a journal. To me, it feels like such an accomplishment to flip back through all those pages that are now filled with life. I've finished almost five journals now. With the start of each one I'd secretly wish that by the time the journal's pages were full, I'd find my prince charming. Hoping I wouldn't still feel alone as I turned the last page.

After five journals I have yet to find my prince, but I've learned a lot along the way. Through this journey, I've realized that ending up alone is one of my biggest fears. I've realized that in many ways I've put my happiness on hold, thinking I needed to find "the one" that would complete me.

I've come to discover that is not the truth. I've been looking in the wrong direction to fill the longing of my heart. Only God's

Lauryn Taylor

love can fill the emptiness and bring peace into my restlessness.

To be totally transparent, those lies still creep in sometimes and discourage me when I see Lindsey, Kayli, and Carmen so happy with their guys. When they are all out on sweet, romantic dates, I'm sitting on my couch in my onesie watching movies. I have to constantly remind myself that if I let my mind dwell on the fact that my prince charming isn't sitting next to me on the couch, I miss the truth that the King of kings is living in my heart. I'm never alone!

No matter where I go (or don't go), He is with me! And that's the best happy ending I could ever ask for...

Do not fear, for I am with you,
do not be afraid, for I am your God.
I will strengthen you, I will help you,
I will hold on to you with My righteous right hand.
ISAIAH 41:10

Why We Worship

If you are like me, *worship* is a word you've have heard all your life. When I hear it, I immediately think of a bunch of people at church all looking at a stage where some guy wearing skinny jeans is leading the group in a familiar chorus.

The sad thing about this image of worship is that after the music fades and the church service is over, we go home...right back to our everyday lives. To be honest, I've caught myself getting more excited about singing a new Taylor Swift song than I have about singing praises to Jesus who gave His life for me on the cross.

Now don't get me wrong, being excited about other things in life isn't a bad thing, but whatever captures our hearts is actually what we end up worshiping. A relationship, a talent, an opportunity— whatever we give our attention and affection to on a daily basis is what we worship. But there is only One worthy of our worship! And worshiping Him is more than just attending church on Sunday and singing a few catchy songs. It's a way of life!

carmen

In Psalm 63:3, it says that God's love is better than life. His love is better than anything this entire world could offer us! That's a bold statement, now isn't it? In response to this, the psalmist says "my lips will glorify You." Notice that it doesn't say "my lips will glorify You only on Sunday mornings, but will focus on other things during the rest of the week." To me, it sounds like the psalmist couldn't help but praise God <u>constantly</u>!

This verse changes everything for me. I want to live like that. I want my whole life to be an act of worship. <u>When our identity truly comes from Christ, we can't help but live a life of worship because we are in complete awe of our God.</u>

That's my prayer for you today!

My lips will glorify You
because Your faithful love is better than life.

PSALM 63:3

DAY 4

Seeking Worth in All the Wrong Places

I think we can agree that at one time or another we've all asked ourselves the question, "Who am I?" There are so many things in this world promising answers to that question but we must be wise about where we look for our sense of self worth.

We live in a day and age where we are bombarded by images and voices telling us what to believe and who we should be. It's not a bad thing to search for answers but as humans, we are easily distracted and led astray just like Adam and Eve in the garden.

God yearns for us to draw close to Him. His presence is the only place where we will find our true identity and value. This is where I discovered my worth and I run back into His arms whenever I lose sight of who I am called to be. I seek the Lord and ask Him to remind me of who He says I am. I find those answers in God's Word and through times of prayer.

God's Word tells me that my identity is based solely in Jesus Christ. I have found myself running around like a crazy person when I forget God's love for me and His calling on my life. Our clothing, cars, jewelry, and nice homes will all fade—but God's love will

Kayli

never end. Jim Carrey, the Hollywood actor, once made the statement that he wished everyone could become rich and famous so they could see it's not the answer. Our worth cannot be found in material things, success, or others' opinions of us. This reality can be difficult to embrace when we want so desparately to be approved. Finding our identity in anything else besides Christ distracts us from the entire purpose of the short time we have on this planet.

There is a God who loves you right where you are. He loves you in spite of all you've done. He doesn't evaluate you based on what brand of clothes you wear, how big the number is in your bank account, or how well liked you are by those around you. He loves you because He created you. Because you are you.

Your worth is determined by who God says you are, and He says you are treasured and more valuable than you can imagine. He paid the price for you when He died on the cross for your sins. In His presence is where you belong. In His acceptance is where you will find your worth.

Therefore, as you have received Christ Jesus the Lord, walk in Him ... Be careful that no one takes you captive through philosophy and empty deceit based on human tradition, based on the elemental forces of the world, and not based on Christ.

COLOSSIANS 2:6,8

Guide My Steps

Sometimes when I sit down to write a song, it takes time for the words and music to flow. Other times I sit down with my guitar and start singing from my heart, and the song comes together almost effortlessly. That's how it was with "Guide My Steps." This particular song was one I didn't think I'd play for anyone else, but after I sang it for my family, they encouraged me to share it.

I still catch myself singing the words and they are a good reminder to me that <u>God has and will continue to guide my steps.</u> That has always been the cry of my heart—for God to lead me and order my steps <u>in the direction He wants me to go.</u> I view my story as a series of open and shut doors. It's a story of me walking through each open door in faith trusting that if it shuts, God has something else—something better—planned.

There's a quote from former actress Marilyn Monroe that I think is interesting: "I believe that everything happens for a reason ...

sometimes good things fall apart so better things can fall together."[1]

Lauryn Taylor

Trust me, so many good things will fall apart along the way and those moments can be discouraging if you lose sight of this reality: God only wants what's best for us, and He can see the big picture. My prayer is that my heart would want what He wants, for His will to be my will.

My prayer for you is the same. I encourage you today to ask Him to open doors He wants opened and shut the doors He wants shut. Trust Him because He is always faithful. Whether that is an opportunity or a relationship or an important decision, ask, and He will guide your steps.

I will instruct you and teach you in the way you should go,
I will counsel you with my eye upon you.

PSALM 32:8 (ESV)

DAY
6

Faith Under Pressure

In so many places in the Bible, we find promises from God that give us hope and reassurance in situations where we feel under attack or in the midst of a trial as Christians. James 1:12 is a promise that I hold onto because of the tremendous hope it gives me.

For a while, I worked as a waitress. It was tough to treat each table with proper attention while also dealing with co-workers who tested my faith constantly. Once people I worked with found out that I was a Christian singer, they immediately started asking controversial questions like "What do you think about evolution?" and "How can you even prove that God exists?"

I have grown up in church my whole life, so I have a solid foundation of truth based on God's Word. But when those tough questions were asked, I felt so much pressure to answer wisely because I knew whatever I said would either point them toward God or away from Him. I just wanted to love my co-workers well (even though most of the time they put me down and made

Christians look like hypocrites). I wanted to help them discover what a relationship with Christ was really about.

What I learned from being a waitress is this: the enemy loves to test our faith. He wants us to doubt it and give in to what the world tells us is true. However, when we love others through our words and actions and stand up for Jesus, the Bible promises that we will be rewarded with a crown of life.

carmen

How amazing is that?!

As a believer, think about how you react in times of trial or persecution against your faith. Let's stay true to our convictions even when things get tough. And let's love others well as we live out our faith!

A man who endures trials is blessed,

because when he passes the test he will receive the

crown of life that God has promised to those who love Him.

JAMES 1:12

created for His purpose

Jeremiah 1:5 is a verse that I whole heartedly cling to. In it, we see God's beautiful words to the prophet Jeremiah, but we also see a powerful reality that is true for us as well.

Whenever I read this verse, I'm comforted by the thought that God knows everything about us and had a plan for us before we were born. Do you ever think about that? God knew about you long before you were even created. In fact, He even knows the exact number of hairs on your head.

He created us to be set apart from this world, which means He has a specific calling on your life and mine. He has a plan for each of us and has uniquely designed us to bring Him glory in different ways. Nowhere in God's Word does it say your life or your calling will be a walk in the park. On the contrary, whatever God calls you to will require a tremendous amount of commitment and a great deal of endurance. But we can rest in the fact that He will give us everything we need to fulfill the plans He has for us.

The fascinating thing about this biblical truth is that our Creator placed a calling on our lives <u>BEFORE</u> we were even born. That's a huge deal! It means <u>we were created on purpose and with great attention to detail</u>. We should be excited and grateful for that.

Kayli

Think about the fact that God made you in His image. While you were being formed in your mother's womb, God was shaping everything about you. He was putting all the finishing touches on another one He calls <u>His masterpiece.</u>

There was a calling on your life before you even graced this world with your presence. I hope you are encouraged by this truth and will cling to it on good days as well as difficult days. <u>I hope you recognize that you are not a mistake. God does not make mistakes. He creates masterpieces!</u>

Before I formed you in the womb I knew you,

and before you were born I consecrated you,

I appointed you a prophet to the nations.

JEREMIAH 1:5 (ESV)

There Is No Impossible

God's Word is filled with promises. When I think about all of those promises, Isaiah 40:29-31 stands out as my favorite. It's a beautiful passage about the source of our strength.

Have you ever felt like you'd given your all at something and you were too weak to try again? I've been there. I was a competition cheerleader growing up. I remember trying to land my back tuck, but landing on my face over and over again. My coach would tell me how to fix the problem, but no matter how hard I tried, it seemed impossible. When it came competition time, I prayed right before we hit the floor and asked God to renew my strength and help me do my very best. I knew in that moment that I couldn't do it on my own. And God was gracious. His supernatural strength took over and He gave me the power to do what seemed impossible!

That's one example of how He has given me strength in a tangible way. But there are many more examples of how He has strengthened me spiritually and given me hope when I felt weary or discouraged. Maybe you have felt like a dream of yours is too far out of reach.

Lindsey

You've exhausted all your options and it's starting to feel like that dream is dying. I've been there too. But I've learned this truth: when we lay down our dreams and put our trust in God's plans instead of our own, He gives us strength to do the impossible. Our dreams pale in comparison to what He desires to do in and through our lives. He wants to empower us to do amazing things for His glory. Even in our weakness, He is strong.

Trust in the Lord and He will give you the strength to soar beyond your wildest dreams! He will give you the power to glorify Him with your life!

He gives strength to the weary
and strengthens the powerless.
Youths may faint and grow weary,
and young men stumble and fall,
but those who trust in the LORD
will renew their strength;
they will soar on wings like eagles,
they will run and not grow weary,
they will walk and not faint.

ISAIAH 40:29-31

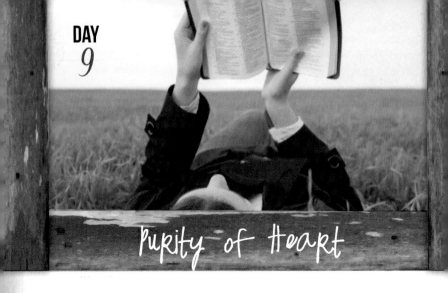

purity of Heart

What does it look like to have a pure heart? Have you ever thought about that question? I'm sure you've heard people talk about being pure in heart, but have you really stopped to think about what it means for your life?

When I hear the word *pure*, what I think to myself is more along the lines of *perfect*. I immediately start to criticize myself and wonder why I mess up on a daily basis.

Over time, I've realized that perfect people just do not exist. God's desire is that we aim to have a pure heart in everything we do. The official definition of *pure* is this: not mixed with anything else; clean and not harmful in any way.[2]

When we guard our hearts, we try to keep it clean from any sinful motives or desires. The truth is that we are human and every one of us will struggle from time to time. But if our eyes are set on Jesus and not "mixed with anything else," we will begin to live differently.

Here are three ways I've learned to aim at having a pure heart:

1. <u>Pray.</u> Ask God daily to protect you from desires and actions that are not pleasing to Him.

2. <u>Read the Bible</u>. It can be hard to find time to read with our busy schedules, but the Bible is filled with life-giving words. <u>The more you write God's words on your heart, the more you will see Him purify your heart.</u>

3. <u>Watch what you fill your mind with.</u> If you constantly fill your mind with things that cause you to stumble in your faith, it will be hard to guard your heart against evil.

<u>Focus on guarding your heart against any impurities of this world</u> starting today! Pray, read, and watch.

carmen

Blessed are the pure in heart, for they shall see God.

MATTHEW 5:8 (ESV)

Forgive

Forgiveness. This has probably been the most challenging lesson the Lord has been teaching me for the past year. Let me tell you that this lesson doesn't get any easier as you get older; in fact I feel like it gets even harder.

This past year the Lord has been really challenging me to pray for those who wrong me. Scripture tells us that the grace we are called to give others is the same grace we ourselves have been given. Since we know for sure that none of us are perfect, we have to come to grips with the fact that we are all in need of forgiveness. And when we find ourselves unwilling to forgive others, we need to remember the grace God has extended to us. Holding onto unforgiveness is a burden we were not meant to carry. We will never see what lies ahead of us if we are always looking back at all those who have wronged us.

Maybe it is not someone else who we need to forgive. Maybe it's ourselves. Sometimes we feel like we've strayed too far. We convince ourselves that what we've done is too terrible for God's grace to cover.  That is not true. Jesus died on a cross thousands of years ago for every sin that would ever be committed on this earth. And because of His perfect sacrifice, we can experience forgiveness that frees us from our sin. His grace changes us from the inside out, makes us whole, and gives us the power to forgive.

Kayli

Forgive yourself; God forgave you a long time ago. Forgive the person who has wronged you, and let God heal that brokenness.

We all need grace. And praise God, He is infinitely gracious!

Therefore, God's chosen ones, holy and loved, put on heartfelt compassion, kindness, humility, gentleness, and patience, accepting one another and forgiving one another if anyone has a complaint against another. Just as the Lord has forgiven you, so you must also forgive.

COLOSSIANS 3:12-13

Boyz

I'll be the first to admit I love **love**! Ever since I was a little girl the idea of being a princess and having a "prince charming" was always the make-believe I dreamed of. As I became a teenager, I chased after that fairy tale and interviewed every potential "prince" in an attempts to find my happily ever after. It turns out some of those guys were really just toads who left my heart with big ol' warts!

After investing years in a relationship that ultimately failed, I realized my grip on this whole fairy tale idea was too tight and I needed to get back to pursuing my first love, Jesus. I promised God that I was going to keep my eyes only on Him and let Him be in control of writing my story. I opened my heart to Jesus, telling Him my dreams and desires, and I spent time learning about Him by reading the Bible. I fell in love with Jesus all over again.

About six months later, I led worship at a retreat with some friends. It was there that I found "the one!" The funny part is, I had known him for years. Austin was my best friend, and we had done ministry together since we met. We spent time praying and worshiping God together. But at this retreat, it was different. I saw his heart. Austin is passionate about everything I love—music, sports, and most importantly, Jesus! I found out later that for months God had put it on Austin's heart to be praying for me!

Lindsey

Four years later, I am married to my best friend and we are more in love than ever! But that didn't happen by chasing him or throwing myself at him. Austin and I were separately pursuing Jesus, and when we gave Him control of our lives, He gave us each other!

I encourage you to give God control of your love life. Don't go searching or chasing after boys! God wants to save you from the toads. Pursue Him and He will give you the desires of your heart; be patient.

Do not be unequally yoked with unbelievers.

2 CORINTHIANS 6:14A (ESV)

Friends & Influences

You know it's a good line when your eyebrows go up, your eyes open wide like a light bulb went off in your brain, and you immediately pull out your phone to capture the words. "Show me your friends, and I'll show you your future," my pastor, Chris Hodges, urged as he spoke to thousands at a conference.

Brilliant. 'Nuff said. He could have just dropped the mic and walked off stage after that. It's simple, yet so true. You will become like those you hang out with. The importance of who you allow to speak into your life is extreme.

During 1 Girl Nation auditions, we had a well-known artist speak to us one morning. She advised us to pick a handful of people to let into our "circle of trust." These are people who know us inside and out, love us no matter what, want the best for us, and will be honest even if it hurts. She helped us recognize the importance of listening to those we trusted over the voices of others who might criticize or say hurtful things about us.

Guard Your Heart

I want to give you the same advice. Surround yourself with godly people who love you and will speak truth into your life. And don't take to heart discouraging comments from people who don't know you well. By surrounding yourself with godly people, you are protecting your most valuable asset—your heart.

Lauryn Taylor

Take out your phone, and write this one down... God said, "Above all else, guard your heart, for everything you do flows from it." Really think about what that says. If everything we do flows from our hearts, then we need to make sure our hearts are spiritually healthy! We need to guard our source of life and emotions with great care.

God's Word is brilliant beyond measure. Take it to heart! Through the accountability of His truth and your close friends, you can filter what the rest of the world may throw at you. You can hold on to what it trustworthy and push aside everything else.

Above all else, guard your heart,
for everything you do flows from it.
PROVERBS 4:23 (NIV)

Depth of Christ's Love

Love...the word that most songs are written about. Love is what everybody is seeking. Love is what makes us feel alive and complete. I have felt the power of love from family members, friends, and experiences like singing on stages across the country. But most importantly, I have learned what love is through my relationship with God. By His very nature, God is love.

There is a passage in Scripture that brings great encouragement to us as believers. Romans 8:38-39 says, "For I am convinced that neither death nor life, neither angels nor demons, neither the present nor the future, nor any powers, neither height nor depth, nor anything else in all creation, will be able to separate us from the love of God that is in Christ Jesus our Lord."

I don't know about you, but when I even begin to comprehend being loved that way, it moves my heart. When I think of a love so determined and strong, it rocks my world. God will not let anything come between His love and those who belong to Him. The depth

Kayli

of Christ's love for us can never be measured or fully understood with our human minds. His love is perfect.

God knows every weakness, every mistake, every wrong turn we have ever taken in our lives, and yet He still loves us more than we can imagine.

God's love is eternal, and the depth of His compassion is immeasurable. So when I say that He loves you more than you'll ever know, that's the honest and beautiful truth. And the more you let His love sink into your heart, the deeper you will love Him in return.

For I am convinced that neither death nor life, neither angels nor demons, neither the present nor the future, nor any powers, neither height nor depth, nor anything else in all creation, will be able to separate us from the love of God that is in Christ Jesus our Lord.

ROMANS 8:38-39 (NIV)

Haters

Loving your enemies is probably one of the hardest things to do. I can remember times in my life where I really fought God on this one. I remember prayers of me saying "But God, she said this about me" or "God, he completely ruined my trust." His answer stayed the same: "Love them anyway." I very clearly remember the times I obeyed Him and the times I didn't, and believe me, holding a grudge gets you NOWHERE. Most of the time, I honestly can't even recall why I was mad in the first place.

I can, however, remember a time when I actually chose love over hate. It was homecoming season during my senior year of high school. I was so honored to be on Homecoming Court with a lot of friends from my class. Surprisingly, I won Homecoming Queen, which should have been an exciting thing for me, but it actually turned out to be something else. Some of my "friends" who were also on Homecoming Court immediately began to hate me and started rumors that the voting was rigged.

For two weeks straight I heard the rumors and saw the mean looks—there was even one girl who pushed me against my locker!

I remember going home to my mom, crying and telling her how mean the other girls had been to me. And as she held me, she told me, "Lindsey, keep loving them despite what they do or say. Hurt people, hurt people."

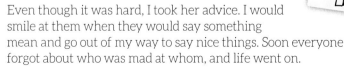

Lindsey

Even though it was hard, I took her advice. I would smile at them when they would say something mean and go out of my way to say nice things. Soon everyone forgot about who was mad at whom, and life went on.

Recently I logged on to my Facebook and had a message from the girl who pushed me into the locker. She said, "Lindsey, I am so happy for you and your music success. I wanted to take the time to thank you for being the only person in my life who looked like Jesus. You were always nice to me and a good friend. Your faith gives me hope in Christianity."

She went on to talk about how a lot of people in her life had let her down and she started to question Christianity all together. I was able to talk with her and encourage her as best as I could. I truly believe if I hadn't listened to Jesus and my mom, I would never have had the opportunity to reconnect with her and show her love.

Loving others is bigger than just being nice; it's showing them Jesus. Haters gonna hate, love them anyway!

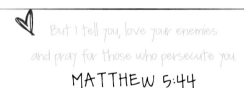

But I tell you, love your enemies and pray for those who persecute you

MATTHEW 5:44

The Beauty of Love

I drove three hours to Nashville by myself, jumped in the car with Kayli and Carmen for another four hours, only to get on a plane in Louisville and fly to Chicago to board another plane to Phoenix, then another to San Jose, Cabo. The day we had been counting down to for what seemed like forever was finally here!!

The sunset weather was perfect, not a cloud in sight. Her white dress was the most beautiful symbol of purity that sparkled as bright as her ring. The flowers were the perfect shade of pink; our dresses flowed effortlessly in the salty wind. Everything went off without a hitch, including the surprise mariachi band at the very end. It was the kind of wedding you see in movies, the kind every girl dreams about.

There was not a dry eye on the beach, including the groom, as she walked down that sugar sand isle. Tears of joy came, not because of the beautiful scenery, the beautiful flowers, or her beautiful dress, but because of the true and pure love between Austin and Lindsey. Without their love, it would just be pretty flowers and a white dress. Love made it beautiful.

My favorite version of 1 Corinthians 13 (the love chapter) is found in The Message translation. The passage starts off by saying, "So, no matter what I say, what I believe, and what I do, I'm bankrupt without love."

Because God loves us perfectly, we can love others in a profound and beautiful way. Ultimately, the love we give and receive is all a gift from Him!

Lauryn Taylor

If I give everything I own to the poor and even go to the stake to be burned as a martyr, but I don't love, I've gotten nowhere.

So, no matter what I say, what I believe, and what I do,

I'm bankrupt without love. Love never gives up.

Love cares more for others than for self.

Love doesn't want what it doesn't have.

Love doesn't strut, doesn't have a swelled head,

Doesn't force itself on others,

Isn't always "me first," doesn't fly off the handle,

Doesn't keep score of the sins of others,

Doesn't revel when others grovel,

Takes pleasure in the flowering of truth,

Puts up with anything, trusts God always,

Always looks for the best,

Never looks back, but keeps going to the end.

Love never dies.

1 CORINTHIANS 13:4-8A (MSG)

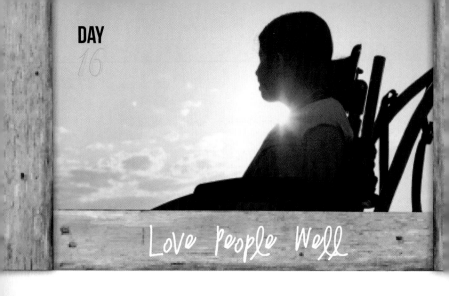

Love People Well

As Christians in our culture today, how do we respond to people who are different than us? It has been a growing trend in music and entertainment to encourage everyone to "be who you are" and "accept your differences" and "be you."

Personally, I love when people embrace who God has made them to be and use their gifts to glorify Him! However, in our generation there still seems to be an excuse not to love people well when they look, act, or believe totally different than us.

Maybe they wear clothes we would never wear. Maybe they are a different religion. Maybe they speak a different language. Maybe they sin differently. See, when Jesus was on this earth, He loved every kind of person the same. Even thieves. Even the broken. Even wrongdoers. Through His eyes, they were all in need of a Savior, just like you and me.

It breaks my heart to see the Christian community completely turn their backs on people based on differences. Aren't we called to show the love of God to everyone?

John 15:12 commands us to love others just as Christ loved us—with a sacrificial, life-giving love. Let's show others what the love of God looks like by loving them deeply and sincerely. They will truly know who we belong to by the way we love.

Pray today for specific people in your life that are hard to love because of differences you may have. Ask for God to help you see them through His eyes so you can love them well.

carmen

This is My command: Love one another as I have loved you.

JOHN 15:12

Authenticity

To be authentic means to be the real thing.

I was blessed to grow up in a strong Christian home with a dad who is a pastor. As much fun as it was growing up in the church, I always felt this pressure to "have it together" all of the time. I was afraid for anyone to see me on my bad days, to know my imperfections, or to watch me struggle. I got so good at being this girl who had it all together that I started to forget who I really was.

I even got to a place where I wasn't being real with God. My quiet times became very routine. I didn't put my heart into anything. I found myself just going through the motions spiritually.

I'm so thankful for people in my life who knew the real me and saw beyond the mask I was wearing. They talked with me about accountability and helped me see the danger of never letting people in. They told me it was okay NOT to be okay! God intended for us to open up with each other about our fears, struggles, dreams,

Lindsey

and desires. That's the whole point of Christian community—to be there for one another.

That was one of the most important lessons of my life. And you know what? I feel relieved when I open up and am authentic. Having friends in your life who pray for you, pray with you, know the real you, and love you no matter what is amazing!

I challenge you to show your friends your imperfections and ask them to pray with you about your struggles. There is power in accountability. It's time to get real.

Therefore, confess your sins to one another and pray for one another, so that you may be healed. The urgent request of a righteous person is very powerful in its effect.

JAMES 5:16

Body of Christ

Without realizing it, we have had to learn to live out this verse as a group: "I urge you to live a life worthy of the calling you have received." We all believe we have been called to this ministry, to give a message to young girls, to start a nice girl movement, and to bring glory to God.

In order to live a life worthy of this calling, we have had to "be completely humble and gentle; be patient, bearing with one another in love." Four very different girls from four very different places can have four very different views on any given subject.

Although hard at times, we have chosen to come together and to use our differences as strengths. We truly want to "make every effort to keep the unity of the Spirit through the bond of peace." This requires humility and grace from all of us as we strive for unity even when we don't see eye to eye on everything.

We know God brought us together for a purpose. I believe He made each of us uniquely to fit together like four pieces of a puzzle. He created our voices individually to blend in harmony. We were all created to come together as the body of Christ. We are His hands and feet. We need each other in order for the body to operate the way God intended.

Lauryn Taylor

This is a picture of what the church is called to be. Every believer is gifted in different ways and we come together to proclaim God's grace to the world around us. God is glorified when His church is unified. This is the life we've all been called to.

As a prisoner for the Lord, then, I urge you to live a life worthy of the calling you have received. Be completely humble and gentle; be patient, bearing with one another in love. Make every effort to keep the unity of the Spirit through the bond of peace.

EPHESIANS 4:1-3 (NIV)

DAY
19

nice Girls

Alright girls. Real talk. How many of us have either been bullied or have been in a group of girls who put others down?

I'd be willing to bet that if we answer honestly, just about every single girl has witnessed or has been affected by bullying. In my life thus far, I've witnessed young girls, old women, moms, and teenagers caught up in the act of putting others down. Why is this such a common thread, particularly in the girl world?

One thing that definitely contributes to this problem is COMPARISON. Comparison will make you compete in your mind with every other girl around you to make sure that you are still in first place. Comparison will make you feel like you have to go to extremes just for people to like you.

Here's the truth though: God loves us ALL the same. The enemy wants us to look at others as different and put others down so that we can be the own god of our lives. However, when we love like Jesus, we cling to what is good and hate what is evil. If we see someone being bullied, hear gossip, or know of hatred of other people, we must shine God's love into the situation.

carmen

Let us be a light into our girl world and create what 1 Girl Nation calls the "Nice Girl Movement."

Pray that God would help you honor others above yourself and to be a light to your friends and family, refraining from putting others down, despite what everyone else is doing.

Love must be without hypocrisy. Detest evil, cling to what is good. Show family affection to one another with brotherly love. Outdo one another in showing honor. Do not lack diligence, be fervent in spirit, serve the Lord. Rejoice in hope, be patient in affliction, be persistent in prayer. Share with the saints in their needs, pursue hospitality.

ROMANS 12:9-13

DAY
20

Diversity

I learned at a very young age that diversity is a good thing and it holds a lot of power. Seeing that I am the only Asian in my family, I learned that having differences is beautiful. My parents taught me that being unique is something to be proud of, and I have always been encouraged to celebrate diversity.

I think our generation is good at embracing people's differences. This does not mean that I think everyone embraces diversity, but I do think as a whole we have certainly made some strides in the right direction. It is no mistake that the Lord led me to be in a girl pop group where our differences from one another is a huge part of what we do and what we have to say through the message in our music.

I encourage you to be the person that is known for loving everyone no matter their background, the color of their skin, or what kind of clothes they wear. Every human being shares a lot in common. We all need God. We all yearn for love and acceptance, and the best love we will ever receive and experience is from Jesus Christ.

Kayli

He tells us in His Word to love one another as we love ourselves. The way I see it is that God is the Creator of the Universe, and He created you perfectly unique. To sit down and truly think about that concept is mind boggling. Then consider that the same God who created you also created every other human being on this planet. He made each one of us with intricate detail, personality, and purpose. We love others and embrace diversity because we love God and we celebrate the creative design He has woven into each of us.

God has called us to love others deeply and to honor them. I challenge you to go above and beyond in showing true love to everyone you meet.

Dear friends, let us love one another, because love is from God, and everyone who loves has been born of God and knows God.

1 JOHN 4:7

our prayer

We are asking that you may be filled with the knowledge of His will in all wisdom and spiritual understanding, so that you may walk worthy of the Lord, fully pleasing to Him, bearing fruit in every good work and growing in the knowledge

...or you...

of God. May you be strengthened with all power,
according to His glorious might, for all endurance
and patience, with joy giving thanks to the
Father, who has enabled you to share in the
saints' inheritance in the light.

COLOSSIANS 1:9-12

51

Contentment

I believe the secret to joy is contentment and the secret to contentment is perspective.

Everyday we have the ability to choose. We can choose to dwell on the things that bring us joy and remind us of God's faithfulness in our lives. Or, we can choose to think about the challenges we face and circumstances we wish were different.

Contentment is all about being satisfied and living life with a sense of gratitude. Contentment compels us to stop seeking satisfaction in our ever-changing circumstances and instead draw near to our never-changing God.

We find incredible insight into this concept from the apostle Paul in Philippians chapter 4. Paul spent his later years on mission for Jesus Christ, experiencing every kind of hardship you can imagine in order to get the gospel to people far and wide. After facing persecution, hunger, material loss, and all kinds of dangers, Paul's perspective was shaped not by his circumstances, but by his relationship with Christ.

Lauryn Taylor

In his letter to the Philippians, he challenged them to dwell on the things of God—to fill their thoughts with reminders of God's goodness that would stir in them a sense of gratitude. He knew that gratitude would ultimately lead to contentment and joy for those who found their satisfaction in Jesus instead of in the things of this world.

Why do we struggle so much to embrace contentment? Why can we not just be satisfied with what we have or with who we are? God calls us to be content because it demonstrates our trust in His provision and faithfulness. It reminds us that our satisfaction is found in Christ alone.

No matter the rain, no matter the storm, choose to count your blessings, or as I like to say, count your rainbows!

Finally brothers, whatever is true, whatever is honorable, whatever is just, whatever is pure, whatever is lovely, whatever is commendable – if there is any moral excellence and if there is any praise – dwell on these things. ... I don't say this out of need, for I have learned to be content in whatever circumstances I am. I know both how to have a little, and I know how to have a lot. In any and all circumstances I have learned the secret of being content-whether well fed or hungry, whether in abundance or in need.

PHILIPPIANS 4:8,11-12

DAY
22

new Mercies

Morning coffee is something that I always look forward to. I love that feeling of being recharged from a good night's sleep and having a fresh start to my day. Though, there are days when I don't want to get out of bed!

Whatever the situation, mornings can bring such joy to our lives when we think about the beauty of a new day. Verses like Lamentations 3:22-25 should encourage us. This passage tells us that God's compassion and love for us NEVER fails and that joy is made new to us every morning. This means that any fear, hurt, disagreement, anger, worry, or mistake from yesterday need not weigh us down in the newness of today. It doesn't mean that we can just totally forget all of our problems from the day before, but we can find our joy in the faithfulness of God and focus on what He has for us in the day ahead.

Psalm 5:3, "In the morning, Lᴏʀᴅ, you hear my voice; in the morning I lay my requests before you and wait expectantly" (NIV). Each day

carmen

is a new chance to refocus. It's a chance to put the previous day behind us and completely put our hope in the Lord.

Today, I challenge you to think about anything that is consuming your mind and taking your attention away from God. Pray that God would refocus your heart and that joy would completely consume your life, radiating the love that comes from Jesus.

Celebrate the newness of each morning and let the promise of His presence give you hope!

The steadfast love of the LORD never ceases,

his mercies never come to an end,

they are new every morning,

great is your faithfulness.

"The LORD is my portion," says my soul,

"therefore I will hope in him."

The LORD is good to those who wait for him,

to the soul who seeks him.

LAMENTATIONS 3:22-25 (ESV)

Happiness vs. Joy

Joy is a topic that I am incredibly passionate about. My mother told me at a young age, "Kayli, sometimes there will be days that you have to CHOOSE joy." Little did I know that small piece of advice would change my life.

It was simple, yet the truth in it holds great worth. Life is not easy. God never promised that it would be. However, He did promise to remain with us throughout life's valleys and mountains.

Have you ever woken up in the morning and immediately thought about the things that you were not looking forward to that day? I think we all have. It can be easy to fall into a pattern of letting anger, resentment, or entitlement rule our attitudes and outlook. God does not want us to walk down that path. It leads nowhere and isn't what He intended for us.

Doing the ministry and having the career that I have, there are so many misconceptions about my life from the outside looking in. I am blessed to simply be alive, and there are so many other great

Kayli

blessings the Lord has given me. However, if I am being completely honest with you, this has been one of the hardest years of my life. I have been in a dark place. I have been in a lonely place. I have been in a broken place where I have nothing but the promise of Jesus. What I have seen play out is God's faithfulness. His faithfulness has given me joy when I did not think I could gather any inside of me. He has given me something to hold on to and look forward to everyday.

Having the joy of the Lord comes from resting in His promises. It is a choice. It's a choice I make everyday. It is so easy to be happy when everything seems to be going right. But, it's an act of worship to praise God through the storm and be joyful when the rain is pouring down on you. I feel closer to Christ when I have done that. It has helped my walk with Him grow deeper.

How about you? Are you choosing joy no matter your circumstances? Let the Lord show you what it means to find joy in His faithfulness!

But let all who take refuge in You rejoice,

let them shout for joy forever.

May You shelter them,

and may those who love Your name

boast about You.

PSALM 5:11

A Grateful Heart

Think about the words *thank you*. How often do you use that phrase on an average day? Is it just something you say because you have to or are you showing your thankfulness by the way you treat the people in your life who bless you?

Being grateful is a lifestyle. When I think about how much my parents have sacrificed for me to be where I am in life, I can't help but be a little disappointed by my actions at times in the past. I've been quick to be annoyed with their opinions and angry at some of their decisions.

Now, trying to do life on my own as an adult, I realize how much they sacrificed for me to live the comfortable life I had growing up! I realize how above and beyond they went to drive me back and forth to Nashville to pursue my dreams. The times my mom would stay up with me until 3:00 AM to help me study for a test I procrastinated on. The times my Dad would leave football games he coached to make it to some performance I had. My parents gave so

Lindsey

much to help me succeed! And I don't think I was nearly as grateful as I should have been.

On an even grander scale, I think about the sacrifice Jesus made on my behalf. He left a perfect place in heaven to come down to a sinful world of people who treated Him like dirt for 33 years and accused Him of being a liar and a phony. He suffered a horrible death on the cross so we could be with Him for eternity!

How do we respond to that kind of love and grace? I think the answer is simply this: we humbly receive the love He offers and then we spend the rest of our lives expressing our gratitude through our words, actions, and attitudes. We live to worship and adore Him every day with a heart that overflows with thankfulness.

I think it's time we live out our gratitude—for the people in our lives who have made sacrifices for us and for our God who has made the greatest sacrifice of all. Let's live a life where we bless others more than ourselves. Let's challenge ourselves to start each day in prayer, thanking God for all He's done and for the people in our lives who love and bless us!

Give thanks in everything,
for this is God's will for you in Christ Jesus.
I THESSALONIANS 5:18

My Story

Some days I look at my life and say, "God, I'm not worthy of how much You've redeemed me and have loved me through my stubbornness."

I grew up in a normal Christian home where my two loving parents and amazing sister showed me what it's like to love each other and Jesus well. Faith has always been a big part of my life, but I'm the type of person who questions everything and has a very curious spirit. Most of the time I feel like that personality trait is a great thing because I love learning new things and diving into new experiences. However, when I was in high school, I started to rebel and experiment with things like alcohol and even went through a phase where I was tempted with stealing.

At 16, I started dating a guy who I gave pieces of my heart to that I should have waited to give to my husband one day. I even had a bad attitude towards tithing and didn't trust what the church did with my money. I was skeptical and questioned everything. I didn't care.

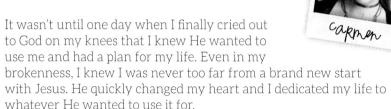

carmen

Throughout this season of my life, I knew without a doubt that God wanted my whole heart. I felt that still, small voice in the back of my mind saying, "Come back to Me."

It wasn't until one day when I finally cried out to God on my knees that I knew He wanted to use me and had a plan for my life. Even in my brokenness, I knew I was never too far from a brand new start with Jesus. He quickly changed my heart and I dedicated my life to whatever He wanted to use it for.

Wherever you are in your spiritual journey today, know that God loves you and has a HUGE plan for your life. Don't waste another minute on the things of this world; draw near to Him and let Him show you how gracious and faithful He is!

"For I know the plans I have for you" -- this is the LORD's declaration -- "plans for your welfare, not for disaster, to give you a future and a hope."

JEREMIAH 29:11

My Story

I was born in the Philippines in a nipa hut, which is basically a tent made out of bamboo sticks with a dirt floor. My birth mother could not afford to give me the life she wanted me to have so she put me up for adoption. The poverty in the Philippines is very high. When I say poverty, I am talking about a country where people live in cardboard boxes or poorly constructed homes; where they are lucky if they have shoes, and it's rare if they know where their next meal will come from.

My parents found out about adopting me through their pastor's wife at the time. The night before I officially became a part of their family, my mom was in Florida visiting her family and stressing out about what to name me. She wasn't quite sure when I would arrive, but she wanted to have a name prepared when I did. My dad was working in the Philippines—he would be the first one to see me and bring me home. On June 30, 1988, my dad called my mom at 1:00 AM and said, "Are you tired?" My mom responded, "Yes I'm tired, it's 1:00 AM." My dad said, "Well you should be tired, you just had

Kayli

a baby girl." That very night before my mom went to bed she had circled the name "Kayli" on a piece of paper.

I love sharing the story of my adoption and all the interesting details it contains, but the part I love most is God's perfect timing and plan. God gave me a beautiful life here on this earth and blessed me with God-fearing parents and a brother and sister who are in love with Jesus too. My parents have been a true example of real love. They taught me to chase my dreams, to embrace the opportunity for a great education, and they loved me enough to let me know when I was wrong. They were at every recital and sporting event. They saved me by loving me...and not a day goes by that I am not grateful to God for choosing to make me their daughter.

Not only am I thankful for this life here on earth, I am even more grateful for eternal life. To share what God has done for me is to simply point you to His character and truth. He is perfect and so are His plans for us. When we place our trust in Jesus, we are adopted into the family of God as His children. I was just fortunate enough to be adopted twice.

Thank you, Jesus, for the gift of eternal life!

For the wages of sin is death, but the gift of God is eternal life in Christ Jesus our Lord.

ROMANS 6:23

My Story

I grew up in church singing "The B-I-B-L-E" as soon as I could talk. My family was always the first to arrive at church on Sunday and the last to leave. At the age of five I said the sinners prayer, but I didn't really understand the commitment I was making or even the words I was repeating. All I knew was that I didn't want to go to the place called Hell!

It wasn't until I was 9 years old that I really understood how much I needed God in my life. My grandma, (who is my hero) had just been diagnosed with cancer and the doctors believed she only had a few months left to live. My world was rocked. I couldn't imagine not having her around and I became angry with God. I remember people telling me to pray that God would heal her, but at that time I had never seen God heal a person and doubted that He was even capable. I remember crying out to Him in anger and asking Him why this was a part of His plan.

But as angry as I was, I watched my grandma go about life with so much joy and peace. I finally asked her one day, "Why are you so happy? Aren't you scared of dying?" I'll never forget her answer: "I'm not scared, because if I do die, I know I'll be in heaven with Jesus. I trust God and His plan for me. I have a peace."

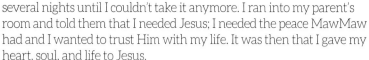

Lindsey

It was then that I knew I didn't have that peace my grandma had. I didn't trust God with my life because I hadn't given it to Him yet. I tossed and turned for several nights until I couldn't take it anymore. I ran into my parent's room and told them that I needed Jesus; I needed the peace MawMaw had and I wanted to trust Him with my life. It was then that I gave my heart, soul, and life to Jesus.

Things immediately changed for me—I had peace, hope, and faith that God could do anything. I started praying daily along with family and friends for God to heal my grandma. Then one day she went to the doctor for a routine check-up and what they found was a miracle! This woman whose body was eaten up with cancer was suddenly 100% CANCER FREE! The doctors said they didn't understand it, but I knew very well what had happened. God answered our prayers! That day God became so real to me, and I dedicated the rest of my days to trying my best to live for Him. Ever since, I've had this fire to tell the world around me about my powerful God who loves us deeply and can bring joy and peace to every situation. Honestly, the sole reason I am in 1 Girl Nation is to use my gifts to share the love and hope of Jesus. Without Him, I am nothing.

In the same way, let your light shine before others, so that they may see your good works and give glory to your Father who is in heaven.

MATTHEW 5:16 (ESV)

My Story

I remember it like it was yesterday, but for some reason I picture it in my head like I'm watching from the outside. I see my four-year-old self with curly blonde hair, sitting next to my mom on my pink bedspread. I know people say that there's no way I could fully understand what it meant to be a Christian at such an early age, but I totally disagree.

I vividly remember going through the drive-thru for lunch one day shortly after, asking my mom from the back seat if I could tell the lady at the window about Jesus. I truly believe God captured my heart at an early age and hasn't let go.

In school I was known as the "good girl." I spent most Friday and Saturday nights at home asking God, "Why do I feel so alone in this?!" I remember begging Him for a best friend, someone else that was like me. His answer, "I want to be your best friend" and that's what happened. My besties were God, my mom, and Wynonna (my first guitar).

Lauryn Taylor

I poured my heartache into songs, and my love for Christ and music grew simultaneously. After high school and lots of prayer, I decided to forgo college to pursue a career in music. Everyone told me it was crazy for a straight-A student to give up a college education for a one-in-a-million shot. But I knew that God was calling me to music.

Fast-forward four years and here I am with a major record deal, touring the world with my three best friends, doing what everyone said was impossible. I could never have dreamed what God had in store for my life when I began this adventure with Him.

After all these years, I am sure of this: He is trustworthy, He is good, and He is tender to the desire of our hearts.

Trust in the LORD and do what is good,

dwell in the land and live securely.

Take delight in the LORD,

and He will give you your heart's desires.

PSALM 37:3-4

Obedience

Have you ever been faced with a crossroad where you had two paths to choose from? Has it ever been really clear which path you should take but for some reason the other one looked way more enticing? I've been there.

To be completely honest with you, there have been times I've chosen to go down the path that was not the best one for me; whether it was a dating relationship that was simply a waste of time, or missing out on a great opportunity that would have helped with my career. No one is perfect. No one will get things right every time, but looking back I can see how much better certain situations would have been had I just handed over my pride and selfish plans, and trusted the Lord.

His ways are higher. They always will be and I'm thankful for that. I encourage you to stay grounded in God's Word daily. I want to challenge you to ask Him for guidance and direction on every decision. Obviously you don't need to approach Him about which flavor of ice cream you should eat! But seriously, His wisdom will guide you in every decision in your life—big or small.

And when you approach Him, do so with humility and an open heart. God does not want us to be human "robots" that obey Him like we have no choice. We do have choices. We have the free will to live our lives according to His Word or to live for our own desires. He wants a relationship with us where our obedience is based on love and gratitude. He wants our humble submission as He guides us through the trials and triumphs of our lives.

When we trust Him, obey Him, and listen for His voice, we won't be disappointed. We won't wish we had chosen a different path. His ways will always surpass our wildest dreams!

Commit your way to the LORD,
trust in Him, and He will act,
making your righteousness shine like the dawn,
your justice like the noonday.

PSALM 37:5-6

prayer

Sometimes people assume that 1 Girl Nation is made up of four girls whose dreams came true overnight. They assume that this career fell into our laps, but that's not the real story at all. We have faced many *no's* in pursuit of our dreams, and even experienced times when we've almost given up. There have been moments when we were so close yet still missed the goal; we've spent years writing and singing anywhere people would listen and have been told over and over again, "you're not good enough."

The auditions for 1 Girl Nation were very intimidating. Every girl was beautiful, talented, and had a heart of gold. But I believe the reason we were the ones standing there in the end was because this was God's will for us.

I remember writing in my journal that week, "God, it's going to have to be You, because I feel so unqualified." We each found out later that the night before the final day of auditions, at the same time, in different rooms, the four of us were on our knees praying for God's perfect will and for a peace with His decision. We know

Lindsey

it had nothing to do with being "good enough" and everything to do with His plan for our lives.

We believe we were each handpicked by God to be in 1 Girl Nation and prayer played an important role in that process. Even now, a few years into this ministry together, we still face struggles but we know in our hearts that God is faithful. Whatever we are facing, we pray together for Him to provide, for Him to heal, and for His will to be done above anything else.

Prayer is the testimony of my life. I know I wouldn't be who I am today without my daily conversations with Jesus. I have had prayers answered with "yes," others with "not yet," and some with "no." I have seen people healed from sickness and even situations in my life completely turned around through the power of prayer. God has listened to my cries for help and has been faithful to give me peace in every circumstance.

I would encourage you to talk to God about anything and everything—your fears, your questions, your dreams. But the greatest thing you can pray for is His will in your life. His plans will blow away your expectations! And His peace will hold you steady through the up's and down's of this life.

Do not be anxious about anything, but in everything by prayer and supplication with thanksgiving let your requests be made known to God. And the peace of God, which surpasses all understanding, will guard your hearts and your minds in Christ Jesus.

PHILIPPIANS 4:6-7 (ESV)

peace

Looking out the van window I see nothing but the blur of my favorite colors painted over the mountains of Virginia. We have a couple days off between shows, but are too far away to go home, so we are going to relax at a friend's cottage in Massanutten.

It's fall. Fall is my favorite season of the year. However, this season of life has not been my favorite. I know, you would think it would be because so many great things are happening. The Lord has given us great success in so many areas—we've been nominated for a prestigious award, we are starting our second record, and we were just on national TV with Kirk Cameron!

So many exciting things, but my heart is heavy and my mind is cloudy. What I love most in this world, my family, is going through a hard time and I'm not able to be home with them. I feel helpless. I feel like I'm re-learning how to fully trust God; how to trust Him with what is most precious to me.

Laukyn Taylor

Letting go of control is not fun or easy by any means, but by allowing old ways to die off, my roots are going deeper and my faith is growing stronger. I have learned through this time that when I choose to focus on the One who is in control, the peace that passes understanding clears my mind and lightens my heart.

I wholeheartedly believe He has a plan. That He will take what the enemy means for evil and turn it into good. Just like when the last leaf falls and it turns to winter, so too will this season of life pass. Soon enough, spring will come. New life and beauty will begin to bloom.

Maybe spring is my new favorite season...

You keep him in perfect peace
whose mind is stayed on you,
because he trusts in you
Trust in the Lord forever,
for the Lord God is an everlasting rock.

ISAIAH 26:3-4 (ESV)

Anxiety

Stressful deadlines. Confrontation. Fear of the future. Money. Fitting in. Conflicts. Pressure. LIFE.

Anxiety can fill our lives until it's like an overflowing riverbank. We reach a point where we just can't take it anymore and the anxiousness spills over into every aspect of our lives. How do we control this anxiety? How do we find peace?

In 1 Peter 5:7 we find a simple reminder to cast ALL of our anxiety and worries on God because He cares for us. Not just a few things, every worry and frustration. I don't know if you are like me, but sometimes it feels like I call out to God only to reach His voicemail and I'm left waiting to hear back! It can seem at times as if God doesn't hear us, but the Bible clearly tells us that He cares for us and His heart is tender to our needs.

Recently, I had the coolest experience that helped me learn about this. I was so anxious about my future. I got to the point where I

caRmen

called out, "God, I don't know if I'm in Your will anymore because everything just feels so stressful! I'm to the point where I need a physical sign that I am still on the right path!" The very next day a close friend wrote me a letter. Inside the letter was a check supporting the 1 Girl Nation ministry! My friend explained that the Holy Spirit had been working on his heart and challenging him to be generous in giving. So he and his family had prayed for me and for our ministry right there in their living room before sending the generous gift!

God hears us. We can trust Him. In His presence is where we find a sense of peace that's bigger than any challenge we face. Cast your anxiety and stress and frustrations on Him. Trust God to work in your life in ways that bring Him glory. Let Him far exceed your expectations with His grace and peace.

Cast all your anxiety on him because he cares for you

1 PETER 5:7 (NIV)

Jesus Is Cool

Our culture tells us that being a Christian isn't cool.

From the world's perspective, following Jesus is all about rules and regulations. With magazines, music, and pop culture pushing against the truth of God's Word, we are often portrayed as weak and weird for our convictions. But I think we need to change our way of thinking.

Christianity was never supposed to be seen as a bunch of restrictions—having a relationship with Jesus has always been about FREEDOM and JOY! Because of Christ, we have purpose in this life and hope for eternity. I don't know about you, but I believe that's worth celebrating.

When I hear people talk about Jesus being "uncool," I wonder how that image of Him ever came to be. Jesus healed the sick with His human hands, He loved the broken hearted and forgave the unforgivable; He accepted the outcasts and raised people from the dead. He died on the cross and was resurrected to give us life!

He's alive in us now, healing us, bringing hope into our hearts, and giving us unconditional love. Who could possibly be more amazing than that? No one compares to Him.

Lindsey

I believe its time to be bold about our faith in Christ. In our schools, with our friends, on our sports teams, and everywhere we go. Let's show the world how cool Jesus really is by expressing His love to others and sharing how He has radically changed our lives.

The time is now. Let's be bold!

But whatever gain I had, I counted as loss for the sake of Christ. Indeed, I count everything as loss because of the surpassing worth of knowing Christ Jesus my Lord. For his sake I have suffered the loss of all things and count them as rubbish, in order that I may gain Christ.

PHILIPPIANS 3:7-8 (ESV)

Be the One

They say one is the loneliest number, and that may be true, but I also believe one can be the most powerful number!

It only takes one spark to start a fire, one drop to start a ripple. It only takes one domino to start a chain reaction. So too, it only takes one person to stand up and start a movement. I know, it's scary taking that first step. You may feel like you're alone, but there are others watching and waiting for someone to be bold and lead.

During my tenth grade year of high school, I felt like there was a huge shift in the priorities and convictions of those around me. The people who had been my friends since fourth grade—friends I loved dearly—began to change. They started using language and having conversations that crossed a line. The direction they were headed, I couldn't go. I had to be bold enough to remove myself from that group and eventually I made the choice to homeschool after Christmas break.

Lauryn Taylor

When I returned to school my junior year, I was shocked to receive notes thanking me for being strong and taking a stand. Some of my friends realized they didn't have to follow the crowd anymore. As lonely and difficult as tenth grade was, my junior and senior years helped me see that I'd made the right decision. The Lord gave me favor and influence those last years of high school and people respected me for who I was. Being bold and staying true to my convictions made an impact on those around me.

How about you? Are you willing to live out your faith boldly?

You were put on this earth for a purpose. He has placed you where you are for such a time as this. Take hold of what God has for you! Stand up for your faith. Shine bright for His glory. Be brave and bold. Be the one.

Do everything without grumbling and arguing, so that you may be blameless and pure, children of God who are faultless in a crooked and perverted generation, among whom you shine like stars in the world. Hold firmly to the message of life. Then I can boast in the day of Christ that I didn't run or labor for nothing.

PHILIPPIANS 2:14-16

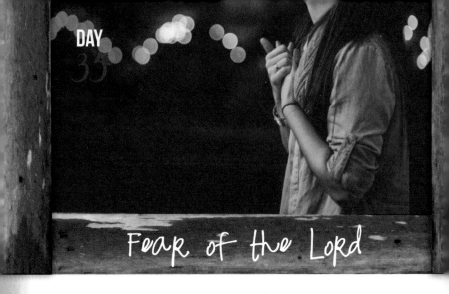

Fear of the Lord

I love the story of Daniel. He stands out to me as one of the boldest people in Scripture when it comes to standing firm in his faith.

We find a piece of his story in Daniel chapter 6. At this point in history, the Lord had given Daniel favor in the eyes of King Darius. He had earned the trust of the king and was appointed an administrator over the kingdom. Daniel's power and authority stirred jealousy in the king's other men so they tried to find a way to charge him with wrongdoing. The only plot they could come up with was to use Daniel's bold faith in the God of Israel against him. The men convinced the king to make a decree that anyone who prayed to anything other than King Darius for 30 days would be thrown into the lions' den.

Despite the fear of being eaten alive, Daniel continued to pray to God and was eventually thrown into the lions' den. Even while in danger, he continued praying and God shut the mouths of the lions.

Carmen

What would happen if we were more like Daniel? He had a holy reverence for God above all else. No death or ruler or even the mouths of lions could keep him from honoring his heavenly Father. The impact of his boldness had eternal significance. All of Darius' kingdom was commanded to show fear and reverence to the God of Daniel.

Whether we are anxious about the future, scared of the dark, or afraid of losing a loved one, let God be the One we put our trust in. Let Him be the One we fear with a holy reverence and unwavering commitment.

We know who goes before us and He is worthy of whatever risk we take to make His name known!

Then King Darius wrote to those of every people, nation, and language who live in all the earth: "May your prosperity abound. I issue a decree that in all my royal dominion, people must tremble in fear before the God of Daniel."

DANIEL 6:25-26

While We're Young

I love that 1 Girl Nation is known for being a part of the younger generation that is living boldly for Jesus right now—we are not waiting until we're older to be sold out to Christ. God has called us to take a stand and that's what we strive for every day.

No one is ever too young or too old to live boldly for God. If we are willing to be used by Him, He will equip us and accomplish big things in and through us. We don't need to have it all together or have all the answers to live for His glory.

The story of David in Scripture always inspires me. He started walking with God at a young age and was even chosen to be king when he was just a boy. God used him in mighty ways but it wasn't because David deserved to be used. He was definitely not portrayed in the Bible as a perfect man, in fact he was deeply flawed. As he got older he made plenty of unwise decisions—he committed adultery and even murdered an innocent man. But he had something that we all need. He had a heart that longed to please God. More than anything in the world, David longed for the presence of God. He was a repentant man who kept seeking God after he failed.

Kayli

David's story challenges me on so many levels. I want to be used by God to do mighty things. And I want to please God in this season of my life. But I recognize that I too am deeply flawed. Being in the type of ministry 1 Girl Nation is in, we have to be so careful about the way we present ourselves. And we have to constantly watch our motives. When we get on stage, the music and lights and dancing is all ultimately for the glory of God. Or is it?

This is the question we have to consistently ask ourselves. It is easy to slip into the temptation to make this about us...to live for ourselves, to use the talents God has given us to further our own ambitions. It's tempting to stay in the spotlight and let people think we're more glamorous than we really are. But the truth is we are human—we have flaws just like David did.

We are called to live boldly for God now, to use our gifts and talents to point people to His love and grace. And we will do that to the best of our ability, using the platform He has given us to reflect His glory. And when we mess up, we will draw near to God with a repentant heart and let Him heal our brokenness.

Though your platform may look different, your calling is the same. Live out your faith boldly in every season of life. Remember that it's not about you. This life, everything you do and everything you are, is all about Christ.

Don't let anyone look down on you because you are young, but set an example for the believers in speech, in conduct, in love, in faith and in purity.

1 TIMOTHY 4:12 (NIV)

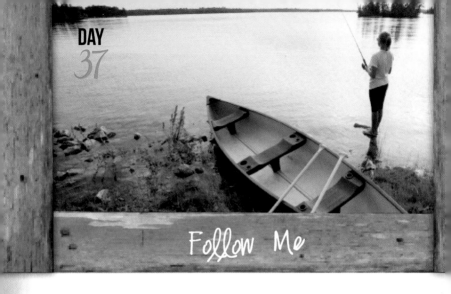

Follow Me

Faith works. Faith without works is dead. Faith takes action. Faith is action. Faith isn't just saying, "I trust that chair." It's sitting in it and trusting it enough to put your full weight on it. It's picking up your feet and leaning back, believing it will hold you up.

Faith is trusting that God knows and wants what's best for you. It's forgoing the plans you made for your life in order to follow Him. Faith is sacrifice.

Faith is beautifully displayed in Mark 1:16-20 when Jesus came to the first disciples: Simon, Andrew, James, and John. They dropped their nets as fishermen, left their families and everything they knew, and obeyed without delay when Jesus said "Come follow Me."

For me, faith is leaving the ones I love for months at a time. It's traveling countless hours in a packed 1999 twelve-passenger van across the country. Faith is trusting that all my bills for the month will be paid even when my bank account shows zero. Faith is being confident that somehow God will show up—He knows what He's doing and why.

Lauryn Taylor

Faith for you may look different. It may mean going to sit by the girl at lunch that no one wants to be friends with. Or trying out for that team you're scared you won't make. Or standing up for what you believe in even if you are the only one standing. Faith steps out and speaks up.

By faith, the disciples became "fishers of men." They got to see Jesus heal the sick, make the blind see, and bring the dead to life. By faith, I have witnessed over 1,000 girls come to know Jesus. I have watched Him provide for needs, heal sickness, break addictions, and change lives.

Trust me, it's worth it. God is faithful. Faith works.

And Jesus said to them, "Follow me, and I will make you become fishers of men." And immediately they left their nets and followed him.

MARK 1:17-18 (ESV)

DAY 38

Endurance

I've been training for a half marathon. As much as I can, I've been running and pushing myself to endure long distances. I even bought an app that helps me keep track of my pace and distance (and I also bought really cute running outfits...naturally!).

When I think about how far a half marathon is, I honestly feel super overwhelmed. Some days I want to take the easy way out and just say to myself, "Maybe I'll try to run this next year." Even though I feel stronger than when I started, the goal still seems so impossible! Sometimes life feels that way too. I look at a situation and say, "God, this is absolutely impossible. I'm trying so hard but I don't feel like I'm getting anywhere!" I wonder at what point I will see the light at the end of the tunnel.

In those moments, I feel overwhelmed and I sometimes question whether or not I am even in God's will for my life. I truly believe that the enemy will try to convince us that we should just quit what we are doing when it gets difficult and start something else.

carmen

However, as followers of Christ, we have to be firm in our faith. When life gets tough, we endure because our God is worth it!

Scripture tells us that we *will* suffer as Christians, but even in the midst of it we can still praise God and trust His strength! I love Galatians 6:9 because it assures us that we will reap a harvest if we do not give up on doing good. It's easy to become weary when we are pouring our lives out for Christ, but He is faithful to give us everything we need to keep going. Don't give up!

We are called to live our lives doing whatever is holy and pleasing to God. We can't give up when life gets tough and the race before us feels impossible. Keep putting one foot in front of the other. Jesus endured the cross for you and me, so I challenge us to willingly endure whatever comes our way for the glory of God!

Let us not become weary in doing good, for at the proper time we will reap a harvest if we do not give up.

GALATIANS 6:9 (NIV)

Big Dreams for His Glory

When I was a little girl, I remember asking my mom about a specific necklace she wore all the time. It was a clear glass ball with a tiny spec of a seed in the middle of it. She told me that the spec was a mustard seed and explained the words of Matthew 17:20 where Jesus said if we have faith the size of a mustard seed, we can move mountains. Nothing will be impossible for those who have faith.

I think we all need reminders like that necklace when it comes to faith. There is always another test around the corner, and without faith, we will be tempted to give up. The hardest lessons in my life have held the greatest rewards.

When I was only five years old, I was living in Italy and I wrote down in my diary that I wanted to, "travel the world, sing for Jesus, and sell a lot of C.D.s so people could know about God." There is something to the innocence and purity of "childlike faith." I believe only God could give a five year old girl a specific desire like that.

Kayli

All these years later, here I am in my twenties doing that exact thing. GOD IS FAITHFUL. God didn't ask me to be perfect before He would use me. He simply equipped me with specific gifts, put a desire in my heart, and honored my willingness to follow His lead. As it turns out, He has lead me straight to my dreams.

Whatever your gifts and passions are, know that the Creator of the universe purposefully gave them to you. If you are great with numbers, be an amazing accountant and do your work as unto the Lord. If you are wired with the steady hands of a surgeon, use your skills to bring healing and do it as an act of worship to the Lord. People often think that if they are not in "full time ministry" then they are not on the mission field. The truth is that if you are a follower of Jesus Christ, every day is another chance to accomplish Kingdom work.

Be a light in your school, at your job, and with your friends. Stay faithful to Him and believe He can and will do eternally significant things through your life. With the faith of a mustard seed, you will see God blow your dreams out of the water!

"For I assure you: If you have faith the size of a mustard seed, you will tell this mountain, 'Move from here to there,' and it will move. Nothing will be impossible for you"

MATTHEW 17:20

He is Faithful

I'm in a season of life when I've had to depend on God more than ever before. Money is pretty tight and there are times when I look at my bank account and wonder how it's all going to work out. And then I open the mailbox and find a check as a late wedding gift or a card from family with birthday money. Those are the moments when I feel the provision and protection of God most tangibly.

Another area of life I'm having to more fully trust God with is my schedule. I just got married this year and there are times when we look at our travel schedules and it seems like so long before we will see each other. But God makes a way and gives us the time together we so desperately need.

God is teaching me to depend solely on Him right now. This season has taken my trust to a whole new level. And as difficult as it has been, I'm thankful for it. These challenging times have taught me more about God's character, specifically about His faithfulness. He is perfectly faithful, infinitely good, and always on time.

Maybe you are going through something right now in your life and you're fearful about the outcome because it's completely out of your control. I challenge you to trust God's faithfulness. He promises to never leave you or forsake you. He promises you a hope and a future.

Lindsey

Trust Him. God works all things for the good of those who love Him. Keep holding on to that promise and trust what you know to be true about Him. He is faithful. All the time.

Know therefore that the LORD your God is God, he is the faithful God, keeping his covenant of love to a thousand generations of those who love him and keep his commandments.

DEUTERONOMY 7:9 (NIV)

Final Thoughts

Thank you for joining us on this journey!

We hope these devotions have encouraged and challenged you in big ways. Over the past 40 days, you've looked at powerful verses of Scripture showcasing God's faithfulness and grace. You've read about His promises and you've seen how He has worked in each of our lives. Before you turn the last page of this book, we want to make sure you understand the most beautiful promise of all... the gospel.

If you are unsure about your relationship with Christ or have questions about what it means to find your identity in Him alone, the next page is just for you! If you already have a relationship with Jesus, use the next page as a tool to help you share your faith with friends and family.

Yours truly,

Carmen Kayla Lindsay ♥, lauryn & taylor

The Gospel

God rules. The Bible tells us God created everything, including you and me, and He is in charge of everything. (Gen. 1:1; Rev. 4:11; Col. 1:16-17)

We sinned. We all choose to disobey God. The Bible calls this sin. Sin separates us from God and deserves God's punishment of death. (Rom. 3:23)

God provided. God sent Jesus, the perfect solution to our sin problem, to rescue us from the punishment we deserve. It's something we, as sinners, could never earn on our own. Jesus alone saves us. (John 3:16; Eph. 2:8-9; Rom. 6:23)

Jesus gives. He lived a perfect life, died on the cross for our sins, and rose again. Because Jesus gave up His life for us, we can be welcomed into God's family for eternity. This is the best gift ever! (Rom. 5:8; 2 Cor. 5:21; 1 Pet. 3:18; Eph. 2:8-9)

We respond. Believe in your heart that Jesus alone saves you through what He's already done on the cross. Repent, turning from self and sin to Jesus. Tell God and others that your faith is in Jesus. (John 14:6; Rom. 10:9-10,13)

CINEMA

THE NEW ALBUM FROM

1 G'RL NATION

AVAILABLE 4·7·15

1girlnation.com  /1GirlNation

Sources

1. "Marilynn Monroe," *Goodreads* [online], [cited 17 December 2014]. Available from the Internet: *www.goodreads.com/quotes/12379-i-believe-that-everything-happens-for-a-reason-people-change*

2. "Pure," *Merriam-Webster* [online], [cited 17 December 2014]. Available from the Internet: *www.merriam-webster.com/dictionary/pure*